PARABLES

LEADER GUIDE

Parables:
Putting Jesus's Stories in Their Place

Parables
978-1-7910-3505-1
978-1-7910-3506-8 *eBook*

Parables DVD
978-1-7910-3509-9

Parables Leader Guide
978-1-7910-3507-5
978-1-7910-3508-2 *eBook*

Also by Josh Scott:
Bible Stories for Grown-Ups:
Reading Scripture with New Eyes

Context: Putting Scripture in Its Place

Josh Scott

PARABLES

LEADER GUIDE

Putting Jesus's Stories in Their Place

Abingdon Press | Nashville

Parables
Putting Jesus's Stories in Their Place
Leader Guide

CONTENTS

CONTENTS

INTRODUCTION

In *Parables: Putting Jesus's Stories in Their Place*, Josh Scott (Lead Pastor, GracePointe Church, Nashville, Tennessee) invites readers to revisit (or, perhaps, to seriously consider for the first time) several of Jesus's parables—short, fictional stories he told during his earthly ministry, which were recorded in the Gospels (frequently in varying versions), that confronted their hearers with his teaching about the kingdom of God. Josh presents the parables as Jesus's characteristic way of engaging his audience's participation, then and now, in their own learning about and participation in God's dream for the world.

This Leader Guide is intended to help you lead a small group of adults from your congregation in a study of the parables Josh discusses in his book. It gives you logistical pointers, Scripture readings, and study questions you can use to plan and lead six sessions, corresponding to the six chapters of *Parables*:

+ **Session 1**: Wine and Wineskins reintroduces participants to the nature of parables and considers Jesus's parable about wine and wineskins as a rejection of "imperial" values in favor of God's values.
+ **Session 2**: The Mustard Seed explores Jesus's parable of the mustard seed against the background of tree imagery in the Old Testament, in order to uncover its meanings for us about hope, patience, and the possibility of transformation.

- **Session 3: The Leaven** examines Jesus's parable about a woman's work in baking bread as a call for us to "show up" and do the work of God's kingdom.
- **Session 4: The Wicked Tenants** considers Jesus's parable about tenant farmers in a vineyard in its first-century Galilean context in order to see it as a critique of authority that prevents the flourishing of human life.
- **Session 5: The Wedding Party** studies two versions of Jesus's parable about a wedding feast to explore the importance of hospitality in God's kingdom, and how the Kingdom calls people to just and creative living.
- **Session 6: The Workers in the Vineyard** focuses on Jesus's parable of laborers paid for a day's work as a challenge to ancient and modern assumptions about God's attitude toward those who are rich and powerful.

Although this Leader Guide is written with the assumption that both leaders and participants will also be reading *Parables*, its quotations from Josh's book and its direct references to and quotations from Scripture mean it can also be used on its own.

Each session contains the following elements to draw from as you plan six in-person, virtual, or hybrid sessions:

- **Session Goals**
- **Biblical Foundations:** Scripture texts for the session, in the New Revised Standard Version Updated Edition.
- **Before Your Session:** Tips to help you prepare a productive session.
- **Starting Your Session:** Discussion questions intended to "warm up" your group for fruitful discussion.
- **Watch Session Video:** View and discuss the session video.

- Book Discussion Questions: You likely will not be able or want to use all the questions in every session, so feel free to pick and choose based on your group's interests and the Spirit's leading.
- Closing Your Session: A focused discussion or reflection, often suggesting action to take beyond the session.
- Opening and Closing Prayers

Thank you for your willingness to lead! May you and your group find your study of *Parables* a worthwhile and rewarding experience that not only provokes new insight but also leads you to a fuller, more faithful participation in God's kingdom.

SESSION 1

Wine and Wineskins

SESSION GOALS

This session's reading, reflection, discussion, and prayer will help participants:

+ reflect on the "unique power" of stories and storytelling in their own experience and in Jesus's earthly ministry,

+ articulate an understanding of parables and why Jesus used them,

+ appreciate the biblical imagery of fasting and feasting that inform Jesus's parable of wine and wineskins (Mark 2:21-22 and parallels), and

+ consider Jesus's parable as a rejection of "imperial" systems opposed to God's will for the world.

BIBLICAL FOUNDATIONS

With many such parables [Jesus] spoke the word to them as they were able to hear it; he did not speak to them except in parables, but he explained everything in private to his disciples.

Mark 4:33-34

Now John's disciples and the Pharisees were fasting, and people came and said to him, "Why do John's disciples and the disciples of the Pharisees *fast, but your disciples do not fast?" Jesus said to them, "The wedding attendants cannot fast while the bridegroom is with them, can they? As long as they have the bridegroom with them, they cannot fast. The days will come when the bridegroom is taken away from them, and then they will fast on that day.*

"No one sews a piece of unshrunk cloth on an old cloak; otherwise, the patch pulls away from it, the new from the old, and a worse tear is made. Similarly, no one puts new wine into old wineskins; otherwise, the wine will burst the skins, and the wine is lost, and so are the skins, but one puts new wine into fresh wineskins."

Mark 2:18-22

BEFORE YOUR SESSION

+ Carefully and prayerfully read this session's Biblical Foundations, more than once. Note words and phrases that attract your attention, and meditate on them. Make special note of how these Gospel stories are the same and different. Write down questions you have, and try to answer them, consulting trusted Bible commentaries.
+ Carefully read the introduction and chapter 1 of *Parables*, more than once.
+ You will need either Bibles for in-person participants or screen slides prepared with Scripture texts for sharing (identify the translation used), or both; newsprint or a markerboard and markers (for in-person sessions); and paper, pens or pencils (in-person).
+ If using the DVD or streaming video, preview the session 1 video segment. Choose the best time in your session plan for viewing it.

STARTING YOUR SESSION

Welcome participants. Talk briefly about why you are excited to lead this study of *Parables: Putting Jesus's Stories in Their Place* by Josh Scott and what you hope to gain from it. Invite volunteers to talk about why they are interested in this study and their hopes for it.

Read aloud from Josh's introduction: "Stories have a unique power. They have the capacity to disarm us, challenge us, shape us, and inspire us. The best stories can cause us to rethink and even change our minds about important things.... [Stories can] connect us to the past and hold our dreams for the future.... Stories are deeply interconnected with what it means to be human." Discuss some or all of these questions:

- What stories (for the moment, other than biblical stories) came to mind as you heard Josh describe the "unique power" of stories?
- In your opinion, what makes a good story? What distinguishes a good storyteller?
- What are some of the earliest stories you remember learning? How important or unimportant are these stories to you today, and why?
- What stories does either your family or your congregation, or both, tell, over and over, and why?
- What story do you most hope people will tell about you in the future? Why?
- What's your favorite story of all time, and why?

As Josh writes, Jesus was, among much else, "a gifted storyteller.... Telling stories...was a central facet of Jesus's approach to sharing his message and vision." Lead participants in brainstorming a list of the stories Jesus told. Write responses (common titles—e.g., "The Good Samaritan"— or key words and phrases) on newsprint or markerboard.

Tell participants that, in this study, your group will explore just six of Jesus's many parables, seeking to understand how Jesus's original audiences would likely have heard them and the often-surprising ways in which these stories still speak to the world today.

OPENING PRAYER

Creator God, the word you spoke in the beginning set a grand story into motion. Its conclusion still awaits us, but as Christians we find its meaning confronts, challenges, and changes us most powerfully in the story of Jesus of Nazareth, your Son, our Savior. As we study stories he told, may your Spirit help us find our place, again or for the first time, in your ongoing story of liberation, renewal, abundance, justice, and love, that we may live as those who are looking for you to bring all things to fulfillment in him. Amen.

WATCH SESSION VIDEO

Watch the session 1 video segment together. Discuss:

+ Which of Josh's statements most interested, intrigued, surprised, or confused you? Why?
+ What questions does this video segment raise for you?

BOOK DISCUSSION QUESTIONS

Side by Side: Defining Parables

Recruit a volunteer to read aloud Mark 4:33-34. Discuss:

+ Josh writes about his father giving him a "for instance" in order to engage his participation in learning important life lessons. How did either your parents or parental figures, or both, encourage your participation in your own learning when you were younger?

- Josh says a parable is a "creative juxtaposition that places two things next to each other, side by side, for the purpose of either drawing a comparison or making a contrast, or both." How is this definition like or unlike other definitions of parables with which you may be familiar?
- Why do you think parables were such a large component of Jesus's teaching?
- Mark says Jesus used parables to speak "the word to them as they were able to hear it." What does this statement mean (v. 33)? Why did—and why do—the parables require additional explanation and interpretation (v. 34)?
- Read also Mark 4:10-13. How do you react to Jesus's explanation of why he spoke in parables? What implications does it have for interpretations of Jesus's parables today?
- What distinguishes parables from mere entertainment, according to Josh? When, if ever, have you felt included in a story someone else was telling? How did that experience affect your response to the story?
- According to Josh, Jesus used parables "to announce the kingdom of God," or "God's dream for the world." What is the nature of God's kingdom, or God's dream? Do you find the images of "kingdom" and "dream" helpful or unhelpful—or both—in communicating this reality today, and why?
- What does Josh mean when he calls Jesus's parables "heavenly stories with earthly meanings"? Review the list of parables your group brainstormed earlier. How do some of these parables illuminate the gap between the way the world was and is, and God's will for it?
- How can familiarity with Jesus's parables hinder our hearing and understanding of them? What, specifically, can we do to help ourselves approach these stories "with an open mind and open heart," as Josh encourages us to?

+ What does Josh mean when he says the stories Jesus told are "fiction about nonfiction," and why does he emphasize this point?
+ "The point of a parable," writes Josh, "is not to be lost in another world but to inspire action in this one." When, if ever, has one of Jesus's parables inspired you to action? What did you do? What happened as a result?

To Fast or Not to Fast?

Recruit a volunteer to read aloud Mark 2:18-22. Discuss:

+ Have you ever had to justify celebrating when others thought celebration wasn't appropriate? How did you do so, and would you do so again? Why or why not?
+ Why is fasting a frequently observed practice in several religions? How does what we do or don't put in our stomachs shape our spirits? What is your personal experience, if any, of fasting for spiritual reasons?
+ Why do people in this passage wonder why Jesus's disciples aren't fasting?
+ What did fasting likely signify for the Pharisees and their disciples, according to Josh? Why did John the Baptist and his disciples fast? (Read Matthew 3:7-10 for background.)
+ How does Jesus explain his disciples' behavior to those who question it?
+ Josh writes that while Jesus's bridegroom imagery "might seem to be a strange metaphor to use,...Jesus's listeners would have understood the significance of the wedding scenario immediately." Does Jesus's metaphor strike you as strange? Why or why not? What modern imagery, if any, might make his point clear today?

- Josh notes that several ancient Hebrew prophets envisioned "the Day of the Lord" as a feast. Read Isaiah 25:6-10a. How does Isaiah's image of the future feast inform Jesus's defense of his disciples' not fasting?

- Read also Mark 2:15-17. Why was the fact that Jesus and his disciples' feasted with "many tax collectors and sinners" (v. 15) offensive to some religious leaders? How did Jesus defend his choice of meal companions?

- According to Josh, how were John the Baptist's and Jesus's understandings of God's coming Kingdom alike and different? How, if at all, do you see these two views reflected in Christianity today? Is there any value in thinking about the Kingdom as a future divine intervention as well as a present reality? Why or why not?

- What is Jesus referring to when he talks about the bridegroom's absence (2:20)? How does this absence illustrate what Josh calls the confrontation between "two drastically different visions for the world"? How, if at all, do you see the visions of empire and of God's kingdom in conflict today? Must these two visions necessarily be at odds? Why or why not?

New Wine and New Wineskins

Discuss:

- What point is Jesus making with his wine-and-wineskins metaphor? How can understanding the process of fermenting wine, as Josh explains it, help us understand Jesus's message here?

- Jesus also uses imagery from sewing and mending to reinforce his point. How is the image of the patched cloak like and unlike the image of the wine and wineskins?

- What other images, if any, can you think of that would help make Jesus's point clear to modern culture?
- Read Matthew 9:16-17 and Luke 5:36-39. How do these versions of Jesus's parable differ from the version Mark records? What might account for these differences?
- Why does Josh reject the "standard commentary" that Jesus's parable of wine and wineskins is about Jesus starting a new religion? Do you agree? How has "setting Jesus up as an enemy of his own tradition" contributed to anti-Semitic, anti-Jewish hatred and violence in the past? How does it do so today? What is or could you and your congregation be doing about anti-Semitism and anti-Judaism in today's society?
- "Jesus's 'new wine' was…a call to his own tradition, and all traditions…to be open to the ways the Spirit might surprise them." Do you agree? Why or why not?
- Read Luke 4:16-21. How does Jesus's interpretation of Isaiah 61:1-2 clarify his understanding of God's kingdom? How does the New Testament say these dimensions of God's kingdom manifest themselves during Jesus's earthly ministry?
- "You can't realize God's dream in Rome's system." What were the hallmarks of and assumptions behind Rome's system? Where do you see systems of "empire and violence" at work in the world and in your society today?
- Where and how do you see Christians embracing or rejecting imperial systems that do not leave space for God's dream to become reality?
- Josh claims the concluding statement in Luke 5:39 "undermines the very core of Jesus's teaching" about new wine. Do you agree? Can Christians ever faithfully desire old wine over new? If not, why not? If so, when and how?

+ "When God's dream is coupled with human collaboration, new realities become possible." When, if ever, have you witnessed or participated in such a collaboration?

CLOSING YOUR SESSION

Invite participants to discuss each of Josh's takeaways from this parable, using the questions he poses (below), as well as to suggest takeaways of their own:

+ "Jesus's followers have a long, tragic track record of trying to advance his vision in ways that contradict his values." How can and do Christians work to avoid repeating this tragic and dangerous history? What are you and your congregation doing to reject "painfully un-Christlike" behavior today?
+ Josh argues the Spirit is moving to inspire "new winemakers" today. Who, if anyone, would you point to as such a new winemaker, and why? How can you know? How do you and your congregation encourage the recognition of "new-to-us wine" the Spirit is fermenting?
+ Josh suggests certain specific practices that can keep Christians "open, flexible, and ready to expand" as the Spirit leads: reading Scripture, meditation, prayer, fellowship, and appreciation of nature. Which of these practices are most helpful and meaningful to you? What other practices, if any, would you add to Josh's list, and why?

CLOSING PRAYER

Lord Jesus, you called yourself the vine, and from you flows new wine that can open us to growth and new possibilities, if we will only drink it. We ask for your help to remain open to how your Spirit surprises us—keeping us open to new things you are doing in the world and in our lives, and moving us to find you in the midst of them. Amen.

SESSION 2

The Parable of the Mustard Seed

SESSION GOALS

This session's reading, reflection, discussion, and prayer will help participants:

+ remember and reflect on their experiences of things of great significance that came from small beginnings;

+ compare and contrast the versions of Jesus's parable of the mustard seed found in Mark, Matthew, and Luke, and explore possible reasons they differ from one another;

+ understand Jesus's parable against the backdrop of selected tree imagery in the Old Testament; and

+ articulate their understandings of what Jesus's parable can mean for us today.

BIBLICAL FOUNDATIONS

[Jesus] also said, "With what can we compare the kingdom of God, or what parable will we use for it? It is like a mustard seed, which, when sown upon the ground, is the smallest of all the seeds on earth, yet when it

19

is sown it grows up and becomes the greatest of all shrubs and puts forth large branches, so that the birds of the air can make nests in its shade."

Mark 4:30-32

[Jesus] put before them another parable: "The kingdom of heaven is like a mustard seed that someone took and sowed in his field; it is the smallest of all the seeds, but when it has grown it is the greatest of shrubs and becomes a tree, so that the birds of the air come and make nests in its branches."

Matthew 13:31-32

[Jesus] said therefore, "What is the kingdom of God like? And to what should I compare it? It is like a mustard seed that someone took and sowed in the garden; it grew and became a tree, and the birds of the air made nests in its branches."

Luke 13:18-19

BEFORE YOUR SESSION

+ Carefully and prayerfully read this session's Biblical Foundations, more than once. Note words and phrases that attract your attention, and meditate on them. Make special note of how these Gospel stories are the same and different. Write down questions you have, and try to answer them, consulting trusted Bible commentaries.
+ Carefully read chapter 2 of *Parables*, more than once.
+ You will need either Bibles for in-person participants or screen slides prepared with Scripture texts for sharing (identify the translation used), or both; newsprint or a markerboard and markers (for in-person sessions); and paper, pens or pencils (in-person).
+ If using the DVD or streaming video, preview the session 2 video segment. Choose the best time in your session plan for viewing it.

STARTING YOUR SESSION

Welcome participants. Ask volunteers to talk briefly about something of great significance—in their personal lives; in their congregation; in the community, nation, or world—that they know of or have personally experienced coming from a small beginning. (You will want to have an example of your own ready in case you need to prompt discussion.)

Tell participants Jesus's parable about a mustard seed, some version of which is present in three of the four New Testament Gospels, is about something of great significance that comes from a small beginning. Read aloud from *Parables*: "The parable of the mustard seed is a challenge to the way [Jesus's] listeners, then and now, envision the kingdom of God."

OPENING PRAYER

God, you have invited us to not underestimate small beginnings. In and through the unlikeliest circumstances, individuals, and communities, you have performed your most powerful works. May your Spirit do such a work in and among us now, as we study, that in this conversation we may hear, welcome, and respond to a challenge from you that will make us more faithful followers of your Son, Jesus Christ. Amen.

WATCH SESSION VIDEO

Watch the session 2 video segment together. Discuss:

+ Which of Josh's statements most interested, intrigued, surprised, or confused you? Why?
+ What questions does this video segment raise for you?

BOOK DISCUSSION QUESTIONS

One Parable, Three Versions

Recruit three readers and assign each reader one of the following scriptures:

+ Mark 4:30-32
+ Matthew 13:31-32
+ Luke 13:18-19

Have the first reader read aloud Mark 4:30-32. Discuss these questions, writing responses on newsprint or markerboard:

+ In Mark's version of this parable, where is the seed sown and by whom? What grows from the seed? How do birds respond to what grows?
+ What is your initial impression of how God's kingdom is like a mustard seed, based on Mark's version?

Have the second reader read aloud Matthew 13:31-32. Discuss these questions, again writing responses on newsprint or markerboard:

+ In Matthew's version of this parable, where is the seed sown and by whom? What grows from the seed? How do birds respond to what grows?
+ What is your initial impression of how God's kingdom is like a mustard seed, based on Matthew's version?
+ Which of the differing details in Matthew's version, if any, seem significant to you, and why?

Have the third reader read aloud Luke 13:18-19. Discuss these questions, once more writing responses on newsprint or markerboard:

+ In Luke's version of this parable, where is the seed sown and by whom? What grows from the seed? How do birds respond to what grows?
+ What is your initial impression of how God's kingdom is like a mustard seed, based on Luke's version?
+ Which of the differing details in Luke's version, if any, seem significant to you, and why?

After your group has heard and talked about all three versions, discuss:

+ What is the most important characteristic of a mustard seed, in Jesus's parable?
+ How does Jesus use the same characteristic of the seed to make a point in Matthew 17:19-20 and Luke 17:5-6?
+ Does the fact that Jesus's assertion about the seed doesn't conform to current botanical knowledge bother you or undercut the parable? Why or why not?
+ Josh suggests the different locations in which the seed is sown—on the ground (Mark), in a field (Matthew), in a garden (Luke)—represent a "movement toward cultivation and control." Do you agree? Why or why not?
+ Josh also suggests the differences in what the seed grows—a shrub (Mark), a shrub that becomes a tree (Matthew), a tree (Luke)—are important. Do you think so? Why or why not?

Trees, Branches, and Birds

Read aloud from *Parables*: "Jesus was Jewish; he was formed in the Jewish tradition...and his life, teaching, and work only make sense within the framework of the Jewish tradition and scriptures." Tell participants Jesus's parable may be drawing on Old Testament imagery of trees with branches in which birds nest.

Recruit a volunteer to read aloud Psalm 104:1, 10-12 as an example of this imagery. Discuss:

+ What does the image of birds in branches represent in these verses?

Read aloud from *Parables*: "The image of birds resting/nesting in branches in the biblical tradition ... is also associated with power, kingship, and empire." Form three small groups of participants. Assign each group one of the following scriptures:

+ Ezekiel 31:1-14
+ Daniel 4:4-27
+ Ezekiel 17:11-24

Instruct each small group to read and discuss its assigned passage, paying special attention to how it uses the images of either trees or birds in tree branches, or both, and what this imagery represents. After allowing 10-15 minutes for small group discussion, bring the whole group back together. Invite a volunteer from each small group to talk briefly about highlights from their small group's discussion.

Have all participants turn to Ezekiel 31. Discuss:

+ What does the towering tree with beautiful branches in Ezekiel 31 represent? (v. 2; see also 31:18)
+ How did this tree become "the envy of all the trees of Eden" (v. 9)?
+ What happens to this tree? Why? What results follow? (vv. 10-12)
+ How do birds and other animals relate to the tree? (v. 13)
+ What does this tree's fate mean for other trees? (v. 14)
+ What other "trees," past or present, does the tree in Ezekiel 31 make you think about, and why?

Have all participants turn to Daniel 4. Discuss:

+ What does the tall tree at the center of the world in King Nebuchadnezzar's dream represent? (v. 22)
+ How do birds and other animals relate to the tree? (vv. 12, 21)
+ What happens to this tree? Why? What results follow? (vv. 14-15, 25; see also 4:28-33)

+ What lessons does this tree's fate carry for other trees?
  (v. 17; see also 4:34-37)
+ What other "trees," past or present, does the tree in Daniel 4
  make you think about, and why?

Have all participants turn to Ezekiel 17. Discuss:

+ What reasons does God, through the prophet, give for the
  events of the Babylonian Exile? (vv. 11-14)
+ Why does the prophet proclaim God's judgment against the
  deported king of Judah, King Zedekiah? (vv. 15-21)
+ What does the cedar sprig God promises to transplant to a
  high mountain in Israel represent? (vv. 22-23a)
+ How will birds and other animals relate to the transplanted,
  transformed tree? (v. 23b)
+ What lessons does this tree's fate carry for other trees? (v. 24)
+ What hope did the tree imagery in Ezekiel 17 hold out to
  God's people after the Babylonian Exile? What hope, if any,
  do you think it holds out to God's people today?
+ What "low" and "high," "dry" and "green" trees do you think
  about when you read God's words in verse 24?

After your whole group has discussed all three passages, discuss:

+ Josh says all these Old Testament images of trees and birds
  "function symbolically to talk about power, leadership, and
  the right to rule the world." How might these images help us
  further understand Jesus's references to birds and trees in his
  parable of the mustard seed?

What Kind of Plant?

Remind participants, as Josh does, that the Gospels shift the kind of
plant the mustard seed becomes. Discuss:

- "In some ways," writes Josh, "a mustard plant is a bit weed-like," wild and difficult to cultivate. What weeds are you familiar with?

- Why would Jesus associate God's kingdom with a weed, as he does in Mark's version of this parable? Do you agree the comparison "would have surely been shocking" to Jesus's first audience? Why or why not?

- "Like mustard, once sown, began to grow in unwieldy ways, so was Jesus's vision of the Kingdom." When, if ever, have you seen evidence of God's kingdom spreading and growing in wild and "unwieldy" ways?

- Josh says Jesus also envisioned God's kingdom "tak[ing] time to germinate and take root." When, if ever, have you experienced the Kingdom taking time to grow?

- Josh writes, "[O]nce someone had tasted and seen what the world could be, they would never be content with the status quo ever again." How have or do you or someone you know experienced or experience this kind of discontent? What did you or they do, or what are you or they doing, about it?

- Josh mentions resilience as a characteristic of weeds. When, if ever, have you seen the resilience of God's kingdom? Would you describe your congregation as resilient? Your own faith? Why or why not?

- Why does Josh suggest Matthew and Luke downplayed or eliminated the weedy shrub aspect of this parable as found in Mark? What do you think of his hypotheses?

- Do you think today's church, generally, sees itself more as a tree or as a shrub? What about your own congregation? Why?

- Josh also suggests Matthew and Luke may have changed the type of ground in which the mustard seed is placed "to de-radicalize and domesticate the message and meaning of Jesus." How so? Do you agree? Why or why not?

CLOSING YOUR SESSION

Invite participants to discuss each of Josh's takeaways from this parable, as well as to suggest takeaways of their own:

* The parable is meant to inspire hope: "Even if it's under the surface and unseen, every mustard-seed-sized action taken with love and a dream for a better world bears fruit."
* The parable is "a call to patience": "Whether it's the state of the world, our own faith journeys, or our relationships, our patience will be a key ingredient."
* The parable is a story of transformation: "In so many ways the story of the mustard seed is the story of our journey toward growth and human flourishing."
* The parable challenges us to hear Jesus's message without attempting to tame it: "Jesus...has invited us to join the movement...of power with, not power over...of justice and compassion, not the status quo and indifference...of mustard seeds and shrubs, not tall trees and strong branches."

CLOSING PRAYER

Lord Jesus, you promised your first disciples that faith the size of a mustard seed can make great things happen. May your Spirit grant us, who would be your disciples today, the faith to see mountains of oppression and injustice and hatred moved, that your wild reign of liberation and love may more fully spread in this world. Amen.

SESSION 3

The Parable of the Leaven

SESSION GOALS

This session's reading, reflection, discussion, and prayer will help participants:

+ reflect on their knowledge about and experiences of baking bread;

+ consider why Jesus chose to set some parables of God's kingdom, such as the parable of the leaven, in ordinary domestic circumstances;

+ explore the meanings and connotations of other references to literal and symbolic leaven in Scripture, asking how they inform our understanding of Jesus's parable;

+ weigh the significance of details about the amount of dough and the woman's action in Jesus's parable, wondering how they may give rise to new understandings of it; and

+ identify a specific way in which they will "show up" to do the work of God's kingdom.

BIBLICAL FOUNDATIONS

[Jesus] told them another parable: "The kingdom of heaven is like yeast that a woman took and mixed in with three measures of flour until all of it was leavened."

Matthew 13:33

Your boasting is not a good thing. Do you not know that a little yeast leavens all of the dough? Clean out the old yeast so that you may be a new batch of dough, as you really are unleavened. For our paschal lamb, Christ, has been sacrificed. Therefore, let us celebrate the festival, not with the old yeast, the yeast of malice and evil, but with the unleavened bread of sincerity and truth.

1 Corinthians 5:6-8

BEFORE YOUR SESSION

+ Carefully and prayerfully read this session's Biblical Foundations, more than once. Note words and phrases that attract your attention, and meditate on them. Make special note of how these Gospel stories are the same and different. Write down questions you have, and try to answer them, consulting trusted Bible commentaries.

+ Carefully read chapter 3 of *Parables*, more than once.

+ You will need either Bibles for in-person participants or screen slides prepared with Scripture texts for sharing (identify the translation used), or both; newsprint or a markerboard and markers (for in-person sessions); and paper, pens or pencils (in-person).

+ If using the DVD or streaming video, preview the session 3 video segment. Choose the best time in your session plan for viewing it.

- Optional: Provide and serve freshly or recently baked bread. You may wish to ask someone in your group who bakes to provide the bread, or you could secure some from a local bakery. Be sensitive to anyone in the group who may have a gluten sensitivity or other dietary restrictions and provide an alternative when possible.

STARTING YOUR SESSION

Welcome participants. If you or someone else has brought freshly or recently baked bread, serve it. Discuss:

- Have you ever baked or do you regularly bake bread? Can you tell us about any especially successful or unsuccessful bread baking you've done, and what made it so?
- What is leaven (yeast), and why it is important for baking bread? What other ingredients are needed to bake bread, and why?
- What makes baking bread different from preparing other baked goods?
- Josh says his mother-in-law "makes incredible bread." What's the best bread you've ever tasted? Who made it? Who or what else do you associate with freshly baked bread?
- What's one thing, if anything, you think people who do bake bread know or understand about bread—or even perhaps about life—that people who do not bake bread don't?

Read aloud from *Parables*: "This process [of baking bread] reminds me that most of the things we enjoy are a combination and collaboration between humans and the natural world around us." Discuss:

- What other things in life that you enjoy are the product of a collaboration between the natural world and humanity?

Tell participants that, in this session, your group will explore how Jesus's parable about leaven uses the bread-making collaboration between nature and humanity "to expand our imaginations and press beyond what we think is possible."

OPENING PRAYER

Creative and creating God, you do not create alone. In the beginning, your Spirit brooded over the waters of chaos, and through your Word you brought all things into being. May our time of study today contribute in some small way to the continuing creation of your kingdom, that we and others may more fully see and embrace the new possibilities for life you offer. Amen.

WATCH SESSION VIDEO

Watch the session 3 video segment together. Discuss:

+ Which of Josh's statements most interested, intrigued, surprised, or confused you? Why?
+ What questions does this video segment raise for you?

BOOK DISCUSSION QUESTIONS

The Kingdom Is Like the Kitchen

Recruit one volunteer to read aloud Matthew 13:33 and another to read aloud Luke 13:20-21. Ask participants to identify and discuss any similarities or differences between the two versions they find especially interesting. (As Josh states, beyond Matthew's use of the phrase "kingdom of heaven" instead of Luke's "kingdom of God," the two versions are substantially identical.) Point out, as Josh does, that in both Matthew and Luke, the parable of the leaven or yeast immediately follows the parable of the mustard seed (discussed in session 2).

Discuss:

+ Why do you think Jesus sets this story in the midst of, as Josh says, "the monotony and humdrum-ness of daily life"?

+ "Jesus centers the action of a woman in this story." What other stories centered on women's action can you remember or locate in Scripture? How, if at all, does this parable reinforce traditional expectations of a woman's place and work? How, if at all, does this parable subvert or challenge such expectations?

+ Jesus centered at least three other parables he told on women's actions. Read Matthew 25:1-2; Luke 15:8-9; and Luke 18:2-5. What do the women in these stories do? How would you characterize these women, and why? How do these women point us toward God's kingdom?

A Little Bit of Leaven

Form four small groups of participants. Assign each small group one of these scriptures:

+ Exodus 12:14-20, 33-39
+ Mark 8:14-21 and Luke 12:1-3
+ Galatians 5:7-9
+ 1 Corinthians 5:6-8

Instruct each small group to read and discuss its assigned passage(s), paying special attention to how it features the image of leaven and what this leaven represents. After allowing 10-15 minutes for small group discussion, bring the whole group back together. Invite a volunteer from each small group to talk briefly about highlights from their small group's discussion.

Discuss:

+ In Exodus 12, why do the Israelites bake unleavened bread before they leave slavery in Egypt? Why does God command them to keep the Festival of Unleavened Bread throughout their generations?

+ How does eating certain foods or meals keep either you, your family, or your congregation, or all of these, "connected to and grounded in" important stories from your past, as unleavened bread continues to do during Passover for observant Jewish people today?

+ In Mark 8 and Luke 12, what does Jesus mean when he refers to "the yeast [leaven] of the Pharisees" (Mark 8:15; Luke 12:1)? How do his disciples, in Mark, respond to what Jesus says—and how does Jesus respond to them?

+ As Josh notes, Jesus's warnings against Pharisees reflect historical concern about "the influence of different groups that were challenging his movement." Can Christians heed Jesus's warning today without perpetuating anti-Semitic, anti-Jewish stereotypes? If so, how? If not, what should we do with Jesus's warnings now?

+ When have you, personally, encountered "hypocrisy" (Luke 12:1)? How did you respond? What happened? How can Jesus's teaching in Luke 12:2-3 help his followers avoid hypocrisy?

+ In Galatians 5:7-9, what does leaven represent for the apostle Paul? When, if ever, have you experienced the truth of Paul's proverb-like statement in verse 9 for yourself?

+ What does leaven represent for Paul in 1 Corinthians 5:6-8? How, specifically and concretely, does a community of faith "clean out the old yeast" (v. 7)? How and why does Paul use imagery from the Festival of Unleavened Bread to describe Jesus's death?

+ In what ways and through whom might God be calling your community to, in Josh's words, "a different way of being," as God was calling Christians in Galatia and Corinth through Paul?

+ Josh states attitudes such as hypocrisy can, like leaven, go undetected until a "communal catastrophe" results. How does your congregation deal with attitudes that endanger the community's well-being? How does it balance concern for the community's health with concern for its individual members?

+ Given the meaning and connotations of leaven (yeast) elsewhere in Scripture, why does Jesus use it as an image that can point to God's kingdom? How might he be, as Josh suggests, flipping a familiar metaphor on its head?

+ Why does Josh suggest that the Roman Empire and those who benefited from its oppression of Judea saw the kingdom Jesus proclaimed as "a corrupting influence" like leaven, "disrupting the social and economic power structures Rome had established"? Who, if anyone, sees Jesus's followers—or sees you and your congregation—as a threat to social and economic power structures, and why?

(If you are leading a smaller group, you can discuss one or more of these scriptures with everyone, using the above questions as a guide.)

Hiding a Small Amount of Yeast in a Whole Lot of Dough

Read aloud from *Parables*: "[Three measures] is an absurd amount of dough for this woman to be baking and would have produced enough bread to feed more than a hundred people." Discuss:

+ Why does Jesus imagine the woman in his story working with such a large amount of dough?

+ Referring to Old Testament passages in which "three measures" (one ephah) of flour appear (the meal Sarah prepares for the visitors in Genesis 18, the offering Gideon prepares in Judges 6, and Hannah's gift at the Shiloh Tabernacle in 1 Samuel 1), Josh argues this amount of flour "signal[s] the presence of God." Do you find his argument persuasive? Why or why not? If Josh is correct, that "that exaggerated amount of flour became connected" in biblical tradition "with an experience of divine nearness," how does this insight shape your understanding of Jesus's parable?

+ Josh points out the Greek verbs in Matthew 13:33 and Luke 13:2 often translated "mixed" more literally mean "hid." How, if at all, does saying the woman hid—or, as Josh does, "encrypted"—the yeast change the tone and meaning of Jesus's parable for you?

+ How might Jesus's words about what is hidden in Luke 12:2 (considered earlier) shed light on the hidden yeast's significance in this parable?

+ To what extent do you think Jesus wants his followers to follow the example of the woman in the story and "hide" catalysts of God's kingdom? Is "hiding" in this way compatible or at odds with openly doing so? (Compare Matthew 5:14-16; 6:1-6, 16-18.)

+ Josh says the yeast's hiddenness emphasizes that "Jesus's approach to advancing God's kingdom…[is] a process" that "takes time," as baking bread requires "proofing." How so?

+ Read Mark 2:3-17 (parallels: Matthew 9:9-13; Luke 5:27-32) and Luke 19:1-10. How is Jesus's calling of tax collectors an example of his "proofing" God's kingdom? What about his calling of another rich man (Matthew 19:16-22; Mark 10:17-22;

Luke 18:18-23)? When, if ever, have you seen someone's (perhaps your own) reorientation to "their stuff" also lead to "a healing in their relationship to their community," as happened for the tax collectors?

+ How does Jesus's treatment of and engagement with "those who are marginalized and excluded" further demonstrate Jesus's "proofing" of the Kingdom, according to Josh? What examples from the Gospels can you think of or locate?

+ "Jesus chose to build that movement [of God's kingdom] by engaging people and calling them to follow and embrace the kind of values and actions that create a just and generous community." How are you and your congregation following Jesus's example?

+ "For Jesus," writes Josh, "God was experienced as a present reality, not a future intervention." When, if ever, have you witnessed or helped make possible a "decryption" of God's hidden but present kingdom?

CLOSING YOUR SESSION

Read aloud from *Parables*: "Jesus understood that while we are often waiting for God to act or intervene in some way, God is in reality waiting for us to join in and participate in creating a better world.... God is looking for partners and collaborators to bring about a better world. The grapes must be pressed, the mustard seed needs to be planted, and the dough won't knead itself." Discuss:

+ Is God's kingdom synonymous with a better world? Why or why not?

+ Does God only wait for "partners and collaborators" who will help bring about the Kingdom? Does God ever act directly to bring it about and, if so, how?

* "We are main characters" in the story of God's kingdom, Josh asserts, "which means what we do and don't do really matters." What is one thing either you or your congregation, or both, have done that you believe "really matters" in bringing about the Kingdom? What is one thing either you or your congregation, or both, have not done that you believe would have, and may still, "really matter" to achieving God's purposes?

* "Our main job," writes Josh, "is to keep showing up, to keep alert and engaged" in the work of the Kingdom. What is one specific way you will commit to "show up" for God's kingdom before our next session?

CLOSING PRAYER

Lord Jesus, help us to trust that, in God's kingdom, no act of love we perform, no deed of generosity, compassion, and peacemaking, however small and hidden it may seem, is incapable of bringing a bountiful amount of your love and life. Amen.

SESSION 4

The Wicked Tenants

SESSION GOALS

This session's reading, reflection, discussion, and prayer will help participants:

- reflect on any experiences they have of either owning or cultivating land, or both, as emotional context for Jesus's so-called "parable of the wicked tenants" (Mark 12:1-12);
- engage Jesus's parable as a narrative without quick resort to common assumptions and interpretations;
- appreciate the Song of the Vineyard in Isaiah 5 as important context for and a potential aid in understanding Jesus's parable;
- consider the economic situation in first-century Galilee as a potentially valuable resource for interpreting the parable; and
- understand how the parable functions as a critique of temple authorities.

BIBLICAL FOUNDATIONS

I will sing for my beloved
my love song concerning his vineyard:
My beloved had a vineyard
on a very fertile hill.

He dug it and cleared it of stones
    and planted it with choice vines;
he built a watchtower in the midst of it
    and hewed out a wine vat in it;
he expected it to yield grapes,
    but it yielded rotten grapes.

And now, inhabitants of Jerusalem
    and people of Judah,
judge between me
    and my vineyard.
What more was there to do for my vineyard
    that I have not done in it?
When I expected it to yield grapes,
    why did it yield rotten grapes?

And now I will tell you
    what I will do to my vineyard.
I will remove its hedge,
    and it shall be devoured;
I will break down its wall,
    and it shall be trampled down.
I will make it a wasteland;
    it shall not be pruned or hoed,
    and it shall be overgrown with briers and thorns;
I will also command the clouds
    that they rain no rain upon it.

For the vineyard of the LORD *of hosts*
    is the house of Israel,
and the people of Judah
    are his cherished garden;
he expected justice
    but saw bloodshed;
righteousness
    but heard a cry!

                          Isaiah 5:1-7

Then [Jesus] began to speak to them in parables. "A man planted a vineyard, put a fence around it, dug a pit for the winepress, and built a watchtower; then he leased it to tenants and went away. When the season came, he sent a slave to the tenants to collect from them his share of the produce of the vineyard. But they seized him and beat him and sent him away empty-handed. And again he sent another slave to them; this one they beat over the head and insulted. Then he sent another, and that one they killed. And so it was with many others; some they beat, and others they killed. He had still one other, a beloved son. Finally he sent him to them, saying, 'They will respect my son.' But those tenants said to one another, 'This is the heir; come, let us kill him, and the inheritance will be ours.' So they seized him, killed him, and threw him out of the vineyard. What then will the owner of the vineyard do? He will come and destroy the tenants and give the vineyard to others."

Mark 12:1-9

BEFORE YOUR SESSION

* Carefully and prayerfully read this session's Biblical Foundations, more than once. Note words and phrases that attract your attention, and meditate on them. Make special note of how these Gospel stories are the same and different. Write down questions you have, and try to answer them, consulting trusted Bible commentaries.

* Carefully read chapter 4 of *Parables*, more than once.

* You will need either Bibles for in-person participants or screen slides prepared with Scripture texts for sharing (identify the translation used), or both; newsprint or a markerboard and markers (for in-person sessions); and paper, pens or pencils (in-person).

* If using the DVD or streaming video, preview the session 4 video segment. Choose the best time in your session plan for viewing it.

STARTING YOUR SESSION

Welcome participants. Summarize Josh's recollections of playing near "Grandma Millie's grapevine." Invite volunteers who either have or whose families have owned or cultivated, or both, a piece of land to talk about their experiences. Prompt discussion with such questions as:

+ Where was the land you owned?
+ For how long did you/your family own the land? How did you come to own it?
+ For what purpose(s) did you use the land?
+ What are the strongest memories and feelings you associate with the land?
+ Have you/your family ever cultivated land you did not own? What was that experience like?
+ What are the advantages and disadvantages of owning land?

Tell participants Jesus's parable about a vineyard, which your group will consider in this session, revolves around the ownership and use of land. Share Josh's observation that, in the Bible, land is not only a practical concern, "a source of both sustenance and shelter," but also a theological concern. Specifically, as Josh states, "grapevines and vineyards…were significant and symbolic, and could be a societal flash point."

OPENING PRAYER

The earth is yours, O God, and all that is in it; the world, and all that live in it. As we read and reflect on Jesus's parable of a vineyard, may your Spirit show us why and how our stewardship of your earth and all in it matters to you, and how we might live on your land in ways that witness to your reign, God of our salvation. Amen.

WATCH SESSION VIDEO

Watch the session 4 video segment together. Discuss:

+ Which of Josh's statements most interested, intrigued, surprised, or confused you? Why?
+ What questions does this video segment raise for you?

BOOK DISCUSSION QUESTIONS

Reading the Parable

Recruit a volunteer to read aloud Mark 12:1-9. Encourage participants to set aside, at least temporarily, what Josh calls the "assumption that we already know who the characters are supposed to represent" in Jesus's parables. Discuss:

+ What is your opinion of the owner of the vineyard? Why?
+ What possible explanation or justification, if any, for the tenants' behavior in the story can you offer? What about the owner's behavior in response to the tenants?
+ What questions does this story leave you with?
+ Josh states the "standard interpretation" of this parable is that as the vineyard's owner destroys the tenants and gives the vineyard to others, God has taken God's kingdom away from the Jewish people and given it to Gentiles who believe in Jesus. What problems and dangers does such an interpretation present?

Isaiah's Song of the Vineyard

Tell participants that, as Josh notes, Jesus's parable does apparently begin with an allusion to Isaiah 5. Invite a volunteer to read aloud Isaiah 5:1-7. Discuss:

+   Who is the singer and who is the singer's "beloved" in verses 1-2? How does the voice shift in verse 3?

+   What problem about his vineyard does the beloved face (vv. 2-4)? How does this problem differ from the problem in Jesus's parable?

+   How does the beloved say he will respond to the problem of the vineyard (vv. 5-6)?

+   How does verse 7 interpret the song of the vineyard?

+   Does reading Isaiah 5 help you better understand or interpret Jesus's parable? Why or why not?

Jubilees, Joining Houses, and Economic Justice

Discuss:

+   How do you define economic justice? Where do you see economic justice today?

+   Read Leviticus 25:8-24. How do Sabbath years and the Jubilee year provide what Josh calls "a societal reset to guard against the gap between the rich and the poor expanding"?

+   What "societal resets," if any, do or would you support to prevent the widening of the gap between those who are rich and those who are poor in society today? How do you think such "resets" would affect you, personally?

+   Read Isaiah 5:8-9. What activity is the prophet condemning, and why? Why does this condemnation come immediately after the Song of the Vineyard? Would the prophet recognize the same or similar activity in society today? Why or why not?

+   Josh describes the economy of Galilee in Jesus's day as one in which the "policies of globalization and commercialization" enacted by Herod Antipas (the Roman Empire's appointed ruler of Galilee, son of King Herod the Great) "led to a prosperous economy for some people, though the wealth was not shared across social classes." How does this description strike you as like or unlike your society's economy today?

♦ Josh says 90 percent of Galileans "lived at a subsistence level or worse. The two driving issues they would have faced daily" were getting food and paying debts. How does this context "[give] a whole new depth" to petitions in the Lord's Prayer (Matthew 6:11-12)?

♦ Josh describes an economic context of high-interest loans coupled with the persistent threat of bad harvests leading to the confiscation of land and the displacement of farmers and their families. How does this background inform your understanding of the pressures on tenant farmers like those in Jesus's parable?

Rereading and Reconsidering the Parable

Encourage participants to keep the discussions to this point in mind as a volunteer reads aloud, again, Mark 12:1-9. Discuss:

♦ Josh asks, "Can you empathize with the feelings of anger, resentment, betrayal, and embarrassment that real people in [the tenants'] situation would have felt"? How do you respond?

♦ "What if the vineyard owner [in Jesus's parable] is…a wealthy, predatory landowner taking advantage of his neighbor to expand his portfolio?" How does viewing the landowner in this way shape your understanding of the parable?

♦ How much of the economic realities of Jesus's day do you think we can apply to Jesus's fictional story? Why do you think so?

♦ Josh doubts Jesus would use "a character who represents the opposite of God's justice" such as the landowner to represent God in a parable. Do you agree? Why or why not?

♦ Josh states the parable "warns about the consequences of the unbridled enrichment of the few at the expense of the many."

Is it also a parable about God's kingdom, as other parables we have studied have been? Why or why not? What does the parable have to tell us that we would not otherwise know, if anything?

Holy Week Controversy

Recruit a volunteer to read aloud Mark 12:10-12. Discuss:

+ Who is the "them" in verse 12, and why are they opposed to Jesus (read Mark 11:15-18)?
+ What was the relationship between the Roman Empire and the temple authorities like, according to Josh? Why did this relationship lead Jesus to oppose them? Why did Jesus not simply and directly oppose Rome, with whom the authorities were collaborating?
+ How does Jesus's parable of the vineyard continue his conflict with temple authorities in the last week of his earthly ministry (read 11:27-33)?
+ How does Jesus's parable of the vineyard critique these authorities?
+ How was John the Baptist's movement also, in Josh's words, "a critique of the temple authorities"?
+ Why is it important to distinguish between Judaism as a religion, the temple as an institution, and the temple authorities of Jesus's day when discussing the conflicts that helped lead to Jesus's death?
+ Where have you seen or do you see Christian institutions and leaders collaborating with powerful authorities at other people's expense? What responses are most effective at changing such a situation?

CLOSING YOUR SESSION

Invite participants to discuss each of Josh's takeaways from this parable, as well as to suggest takeaways of their own:

+ Josh urges readers to reject the violent, absentee landlord of the parable as an image for God. Do you agree that this image presents more problematic than helpful assumptions about God? Why or why not?

+ Josh argues the separation of politics, economics, and religion "is a myth we have told ourselves to insulate us from the cognitive dissonance that arises when we hear the words of Jesus, but find them too difficult." How do your religious beliefs affect and shape your political and economic ideas? Do you hear Jesus calling you to make difficult but crucial changes? If so, how are you responding? If not, why not?

+ Josh highlights how Jesus chose a nonviolent response to the Roman Empire and its collaborators: "It is not easy, but it is what makes for peace, justice, and a transformed world." When and how have you seen the way of nonviolence make a difference for peace and justice? How are you and your congregation involved in nonviolent work for peace and justice today?

CLOSING PRAYER

Christ Jesus, the good news of your life, death, and resurrection are the cornerstone of our faith. May we build upon that in order to further justice and peace. May your Spirit make us bold to embrace you and your ways, that we may work toward the world of which God dreams. Amen.

SESSION 5

The Wedding Party

SESSION GOALS

This session's reading, reflection, discussion, and prayer will help participants:

+ reflect on their experiences of memorable shared meals as emotional background for interpreting Jesus's parables of great feasts,
+ consider the parable of the great feast in Luke 14 as a story about the relationship of hospitality to God's kingdom, and
+ consider the parable of the wedding banquet in Matthew 22 as a story about "opting out" of prevailing values and economics in favor of creative and just living.

BIBLICAL FOUNDATIONS

Then Jesus said to him, "Someone gave a great dinner and invited many. At the time for the dinner he sent his slave to say to those who had been invited, 'Come, for everything is ready now.' But they all alike began to make excuses. The first said to him, 'I have bought a piece of land, and I must go out and see it; please accept my regrets.' Another said, 'I have bought five yoke of oxen, and I am going to try them out; please accept my regrets.' Another said, 'I have just been married, and therefore I cannot come.' So the slave returned and reported this to his master. Then the owner of the house became angry and said to his slave, 'Go out at once into the streets and lanes of the town and bring in the poor, the crippled, the blind, and the lame.' And the slave said, 'Sir, what you ordered has been done, and there is still room.' Then the master said to the slave, 'Go out into the roads and lanes, and compel people to come in, so that my house may be filled. For I tell you, none of those who were invited will taste my dinner.'"

Luke 14:16-24

Once more Jesus spoke to them in parables, saying: "The kingdom of heaven may be compared to a king who gave a wedding banquet for his son. He sent his slaves to call those who had been invited to the wedding banquet, but they would not come. Again he sent other slaves, saying, 'Tell those who have been invited: Look, I have prepared my dinner, my oxen and my fat calves have been slaughtered, and everything is ready; come to the wedding banquet.' But they made light of it and went away, one to his farm, another to his business, while the rest seized his slaves, mistreated them, and killed them. The king was enraged. He sent his troops, destroyed those murderers, and burned their city. Then he said to his slaves, 'The wedding is ready, but those invited were not worthy. Go therefore into the main streets, and invite everyone you find to the wedding banquet.' Those slaves went out into the streets and gathered all whom they found, both good and bad, so the wedding hall was filled with guests.

"But when the king came in to see the guests, he noticed a man there who was not wearing a wedding robe, and he said to him, 'Friend, how did you get in here without a wedding robe?' And he was speechless. Then the king said to the attendants, 'Bind him hand and foot, and throw him into the outer darkness, where there will be weeping and gnashing of teeth.' For many are called, but few are chosen."

Matthew 22:1-14

BEFORE YOUR SESSION

- Carefully and prayerfully read this session's Biblical Foundations, more than once. Note words and phrases that attract your attention, and meditate on them. Make special note of how these Gospel stories are the same and different. Write down questions you have, and try to answer them, consulting trusted Bible commentaries.
- Carefully read chapter 5 of *Parables*, more than once.
- You will need either Bibles for in-person participants or screen slides prepared with Scripture texts for sharing (identify the translation used), or both; newsprint or a markerboard and markers (for in-person sessions); and paper, pens or pencils (in-person).
- If using the DVD or streaming video, preview the session 5 video segment. Choose the best time in your session plan for viewing it.

STARTING YOUR SESSION

Welcome participants. Ask volunteers to talk briefly about memorable dinner parties (or comparable occasions) they have either attended or hosted, or both. Discuss:

- What made this dinner party such a memorable experience?
- What do you (or what would you) consider the most important thing about a dinner party when attending one? When hosting one?
- Have you ever felt embarrassed or shamed at a dinner party? Why?
- Have you ever refused a dinner invitation you would have liked to have accepted—or accepted one you would have liked to refuse? Why?

- What, if anything, do you think who you choose to have dinner with says about who you are?

Tell participants that, in this session, your group will explore two versions of a parable Jesus told about a dinner party. Read aloud from *Parables*: "[The stories] are related, but obviously not identical, like fraternal twins....It's evident that the same general story is beneath the two versions, a story about a feast and invited guests who refuse to attend, but there are also several differences."

OPENING PRAYER

Great God, you have never been so high and holy as to refuse to eat with your people. From visiting Abraham beneath the oaks to dining with Moses and the elders at Sinai to sharing bread and wine with Jesus's disciples, you have graciously called all people to the table. As we turn our attention to the words of Jesus in this time of study, we ask that what we hear and see in Scripture, from each other, and in our hearts may strengthen us in your service, for the sake of the world you love. Amen.

WATCH SESSION VIDEO

Watch the session 5 video segment together. Discuss:

- Which of Josh's statements most interested, intrigued, surprised, or confused you? Why?
- What questions does this video segment raise for you?

BOOK DISCUSSION QUESTIONS

The Parable of the Great Feast (Luke 14)

Recruit volunteers to read aloud Luke 14:16-24, taking the roles of the narrator (Jesus), the slave, the master, and the three invited guests who make excuses. Discuss:

+ What most interests or confuses you about this story? Why?
+ Who is giving the dinner party in this story, and why?
+ Why do the invited guests refuse to attend?
+ How does the person giving the feast respond when the invitation is refused? What do you think about this response?
+ Josh says, at one level, this story is about "hospitality and social embarrassment." How so? How does the setting in which Jesus tells this story (14:7-14) support this understanding of it?
+ Whom does Jesus say people should invite to banquets, and why? Are his instructions still relevant in today's society? Are they relevant to you and your congregation? Why or why not?
+ A fellow dinner guest's comment about the kingdom of God prompts Jesus to tell this story (v. 15). "As a general rule," Josh writes, "if Jesus responds to something you say or do with a parable, you are probably in trouble." What "trouble," if any, do you think this guest's comment shows he is in? Do you think you have ever been in similar "trouble"? Why or why not?
+ "If those who eat in the Kingdom are blessed, then why not invite them to dinner now? The very act of doing so brings the Kingdom into the present." How did the meals Jesus shared in his ministry bring the Kingdom into the present? When and how, if ever, have either you or your congregation, or both, seen a shared meal do so?

The Parable of the Wedding Banquet (Matthew 22)

Recruit volunteers to read aloud Matthew 22:2-14, taking the roles of the narrator (Jesus), the king, and the guest without a robe. Discuss:

+ What immediately interests or confuses you most about this story? Why?
+ Who is giving the dinner party in this story, and why?

- Why do the invited guests refuse to attend?

- How does the king respond when the invitation is refused? What do you think about this response?

- Why does the king expel the "friend" (v. 12) found at the wedding feast without a wedding garment?

- Is the refusal to attend the feast in Matthew's version of the parable a lesser, greater, or equal offense when compared with the refusal to attend the feast in Luke's version? Why?

- Josh summarizes and rejects "the standard interpretation" of this parable as an allegory of supposed Jewish exclusion from and non-Jewish inclusion in God's kingdom. How has this problematic "replacement theology" interpretation fueled and continued to fuel anti-Semitic, anti-Jewish attitudes and actions?

- Why does Josh reject the suggestion that the king in Jesus's story represents God? Do you agree with him? Why or why not?

- When and how have Christians concluded (as Josh states, summarizing the idea to reject it), "If God is violent then, as God's image bearers, we can be too"?

- If, as Josh argues, God does not "need to resort to violence to get the job done," how should we understand texts in both the Old and New Testaments that depict divine violence?

- How does Josh interpret Jesus's parable about the father and his two sons in Luke 15:11-32 to show God's character in a way he argues this parable does not? If male authority figures from Jesus's parables whom we find disagreeable or dangerous don't always represent God, as Josh argues they don't, can or should we assume male authority figures in the parables whom we find more agreeable do? Why or why not?

- Discussing Matthew 11:12, Josh writes, "There is a violent response to the Kingdom message, not a Kingdom message advanced with violence." When and how have you seen the message of God's reign provoke a violent response? What have either you or your congregation, or both, done about such responses?
- As Josh notes, in Matthew's version, Jesus tells this parable during the events of Holy Week and during a controversy about the source of Jesus's authority to pronounce judgment against the temple leadership. Read Matthew 22:15-22. How does this dispute about paying taxes reflect the same context? How does Jesus demonstrate a choice "to opt out of the system altogether," as Josh says he does, and how does Jesus's choice influence your understanding of the parable?
- "Jesus's Kingdom vision was about realizing the justice and enough-ness that are God's dream for the world, and to do that it would require a radical break with the values of empire, including the economy." To what extent and how, concretely, can Jesus's followers today "break with" or "opt out" from society's values and economics?
- How is the improperly dressed guest (vv. 11-12) opting out of imperial social values and economics? Why does Josh argue this guest "is Jesus himself"? (Compare verse 12b with Matthew 27:14.)
- Who are the "many" and the "few" in Jesus's concluding statement (v. 14)?
- "What [Rome] couldn't fathom were those who chose nonviolence and sought to live in creative and just ways, even when it cost them everything." Where and how do you see people paying the cost of nonviolent resistance to and rejection of social values and economics today?

+ "I propose we start looking for Jesus in his stories by first finding those who are suffering, being excluded, or punished." Why does Josh make this proposal? How, if at all, would it change your understanding of other parables Jesus told? How would, or how does, looking for Jesus in those around us who are suffering, excluded, or punished change our relationships to them?

CLOSING YOUR SESSION

Invite participants to discuss Josh's takeaways from this parable, as well as to suggest takeaways of their own. If desired, use one or more of the questions Josh asks at the conclusion of chapter 5:

+ How does what we buy and where impact those who make those items?
+ With whom am I collaborating and is that good for me, my neighbor, or the world?
+ Is my participation in x, y, and z helping realize God's dream, or is it perpetuating a human nightmare?
+ Am I willing to begin changing the way I manage my excess if it would mean the opportunity for others to have enough?
+ Within the metaphor created by the parable, what are the ill-fitting wedding garments that I need to shed?

CLOSING PRAYER

Lord Jesus, may the message we have encountered here nurture and nourish us as we go into the world you love, and may your Spirit sustain us as we invite all around us—those we regard as good or bad, whether we think them in high places or low—to taste and see your goodness for themselves, experiencing God's great feast realized here and now in fellowship with you and with one another. Amen.

SESSION 6

The Workers in the Vineyard

SESSION GOALS

This session's reading, reflection, discussion, and prayer will help participants:

+ reflect on experiences they have had of either being paid unsatisfactory wages or of exercising responsibility for another person's wages, or both;
+ explore Jesus's parable of the workers in the vineyard (Matthew 20:1-16) as a call to think economically about God's kingdom; and
+ examine how Jesus's encounter with a rich man (Matthew 19:16-30) challenges ancient and modern assumptions about the wealthy and powerful, and may enhance understanding of the parable that follows it.

BIBLICAL FOUNDATION

"For the kingdom of heaven is like a landowner who went out early in the morning to hire laborers for his vineyard. After agreeing with the laborers for a denarius for the day, he sent them into his vineyard. When he went

out about nine o'clock, he saw others standing idle in the marketplace, and he said to them, 'You also go into the vineyard, and I will pay you whatever is right.' So they went. When he went out again about noon and about three o'clock, he did the same. And about five o'clock he went out and found others standing around, and he said to them, 'Why are you standing here idle all day?' They said to him, 'Because no one has hired us.' He said to them, 'You also go into the vineyard.' When evening came, the owner of the vineyard said to his manager, 'Call the laborers and give them their pay, beginning with the last and then going to the first.' When those hired about five o'clock came, each of them received a denarius. Now when the first came, they thought they would receive more; but each of them also received a denarius. And when they received it, they grumbled against the landowner, saying, 'These last worked only one hour, and you have made them equal to us who have borne the burden of the day and the scorching heat.' But he replied to one of them, 'Friend, I am doing you no wrong; did you not agree with me for a denarius? Take what belongs to you and go; I choose to give to this last the same as I give to you. Am I not allowed to do what I choose with what belongs to me? Or are you envious because I am generous?' So the last will be first, and the first will be last."

Matthew 20:1-16

BEFORE YOUR SESSION

- Carefully and prayerfully read this session's Biblical Foundation, more than once. Note words and phrases that attract your attention, and meditate on them. Make special note of how these Gospel stories are the same and different. Write down questions you have, and try to answer them, consulting trusted Bible commentaries.
- Carefully read chapter 6 of *Parables*, more than once.
- You will need either Bibles for in-person participants or screen slides prepared with Scripture texts for sharing (identify the translation used), or both; newsprint or a markerboard and markers (for in-person sessions); and paper, pens or pencils (in-person).

+ If using the DVD or streaming video, preview the session 6 video segment. Choose the best time in your session plan for viewing it.

STARTING YOUR SESSION

Welcome participants. Discuss:

+ What are the strongest memories you have of your first job? Of your first time being paid?
+ Have you ever been dissatisfied enough with your pay to raise the issue with your employer? What happened?
+ Have you ever been in a position to decide what someone else should be paid? If so, how did you exercise that responsibility?
+ What, if anything, do you think Christian faith has to say about paying someone for their labor?

Read aloud from *Parables*: "When it comes to Jesus's stories, or any other part of faith or theology, I find most people don't think economically.…Economics are a kind of lived theology. How the world is carved up, how people do or do not have access to daily bread, are not just about the economy. They are commentary on and the result of what we ultimately believe about God's dream for the world."

Tell participants that, in this final session, your group will study another of Jesus's parables that calls us to think economically about God's kingdom.

OPENING PRAYER

Generous God, who owns the whole creation and can do with it what you please, it has pleased you to set us in the world as stewards who bear your image, tending and caring for what you have made. As we again turn to your Son's teaching about your reign, may your Spirit equip us to listen attentively, ask questions faithfully, and discover clearly your will for human life, that we may then act boldly and obediently. Amen.

WATCH SESSION VIDEO

Watch the session 6 video segment together. Discuss:

+ Which of Josh's statements most interested, intrigued, surprised, or confused you? Why?
+ What questions does this video segment raise for you?

BOOK DISCUSSION QUESTIONS

Controversy in the Vineyard

Recruit volunteers to read aloud Matthew 20:1-16, taking the roles of the narrator (Jesus), the landowner, the laborers hired at the start of the day, those hired at five o'clock, and the manager (vv. 13-15). Discuss:

+ What immediately interests or confuses you most about this story? Why?
+ Which character(s) in the story do you either most relate to or empathize with, or both, and why?
+ How is this story about labor in a vineyard like and unlike the story Jesus tells in Matthew 21:33-40? What, if anything, do these similarities and differences suggest to you about what these stories mean?
+ What is the anti-Semitic, anti-Jewish "interpretive assumption" about this parable that Josh warns against? Why is it important for Christians to be aware of and avoid this interpretation?
+ Why does Josh argue that in this parable (as in 21:33-40), the landowner is not meant to be an image of God? Do you agree? Why or why not?

+ Why does the landowner not hire as many workers as he will need all at once, at the beginning of the day?

+ Why does Josh compare the denarius the landowner agrees to pay to the US minimum wage?

+ Why does the landowner assume the people he hires at nine o'clock and five o'clock have been "idle" (vv. 3, 6)? What do you think of the explanation the latter group gives him (v. 7)?

+ Why does the landowner instruct his manager to distribute the wages to the laborers? How do you imagine the story might sound or actually be different if the manager distributed the wages himself?

+ How much or how little do you empathize with the expectation (v. 10) and the complaint (vv. 11-12) of the laborers who were hired first? Why?

+ What do you think about the explanation the landowner (through his manager) gives to the dissatisfied laborers? Do you agree with Josh that is a form of "gaslighting"? Why or why not?

+ The landowner points out (in the original Greek of v. 15) that what he does is lawful. Josh states, "We all know that there is a difference between what is legal and what is just." When, if ever, have you experienced this difference for yourself? What, if anything, did or could you do in response?

+ Why does the landowner think of the dissatisfied laborers as "envious" and himself as "generous" (v. 15; Greek, "good")? How much do you agree with his assessments, and why? Do you think laborers hired later in the day agreed with his assessments? Why or why not?

+ Josh says the landowner's practices "could ultimately end up pitting the workers against one another." How so? When, if ever, have you seen employers' practices, intentionally or not, create division among employees?

- How does this story illustrate Jesus's saying about "the first" and "the last" (v. 16; compare Matthew 19:30; Mark 10:31; Luke 13:30)? Do you hear Jesus's statement as good news or bad in the context of this parable?

Rich Men and God's Kingdom

Tell participants Josh suggests we can appreciate why Jesus told this parable by looking back at its immediate context. Recruit volunteers to read aloud Matthew 19:16-30, taking the roles of the narrator, Jesus, the rich man, "the disciples" (v. 25), and Peter. Discuss:

- Why does Jesus tell this man to sell his possessions? Why does the man react with sadness to what Jesus says?
- "Possessing wealth in the first century was not a morally neutral act." What moral issues does this man's wealth raise? How are his possessions interfering with his own and with his neighbors' participation in God's kingdom?
- What do you believe to be the moral consequences of possessing wealth today? How do what you and your congregation own get in the way of your and other people's participation in God's kingdom? What are you willing to do in response?
- How, if at all, can possessing wealth support participation in God's kingdom, instead of obstruct it? Does this potential undercut Jesus's teaching about the difficulty of rich people entering God's kingdom (vv. 23-24)? Why or why not?
- The disciples' reaction to Jesus's teaching reflects the ancient world's understanding, in Josh's words, "that the gods were on the side of the rich and powerful, evidenced by the fact that they were rich and powerful." How and why does society today adopt a similar view of the social and economic status quo? What, if anything, are either you

or your congregation, or both, doing to challenge such an understanding, as Jesus challenged it?

+ What motivates Peter's response to Jesus in verse 27? Do you, as Josh does, read Jesus's reply as reassuring and encouraging words? Why or why not? (Compare Mark 10:29-30.)

+ How does this story illustrate Jesus's saying about "the first" and "the last" (v. 30)? Do you hear Jesus's statement as good news or bad in the context of this incident?

+ How, if at all, does this incident inform or change your understanding of Jesus's parable that follows it about the vineyard workers?

+ Do you imagine the rich man ever eventually heeded Jesus's instructions to him? Why or why not?

CLOSING YOUR SESSION

Invite participants to discuss Josh's takeaways from this parable, as well as to suggest takeaways of their own:

+ "The standard reading of this parable...turns the oppressed into the villains of the story, while letting the actual villains off the hook." How can we read Jesus's story in ways that both place responsibility for unjust social and economic systems where they belong, and motivate changes that will encourage greater participation in God's kingdom?

+ "Peace, stability, and...enough-ness...are the markers of God's dream for the world fulfilled." Josh sees these markers in Micah's vision of all people sitting "under their own vines and under their own fig trees" (4:4). What are you and your congregation doing, or what could you do, to promote peace, stability, and "enough-ness" in your community? In the nation? In the world?

61

Thank participants for having studied *Parables* with you. Invite volunteers to talk briefly about what they appreciate or will remember most about either the study, or what questions they still have and the next steps they will take to find answers, or both. Be ready to answer these questions yourself, to model and prompt discussion.

CLOSING PRAYER

Lord Jesus, we thank you for the stories you told—your entertaining, often confounding, sometimes distressing, always demanding stories about God's kingdom. May what we have read and heard in these sessions be more than mere head knowledge. By your grace and by your Spirit, may your stories come alive in us, individually and together as your people, that your reign may take larger and clearer shape among and through us, that more people may know the justice, abundance, and love of life in your presence, here and now. Amen.

Watch videos based on *Parables: Putting Jesus's Stories in their Place* with Josh Scott through Amplify Media.

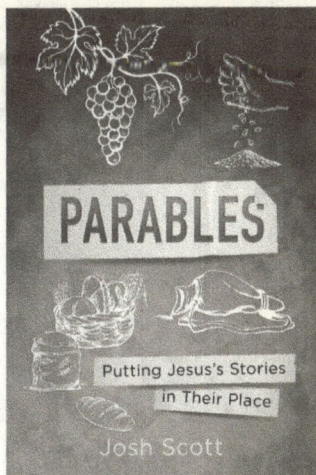

Amplify Media is a multimedia platform that delivers high quality, searchable content with an emphasis on Wesleyan perspectives for churchwide, group, or individual use on any device at any time. In a world of sometimes overwhelming choices, Amplify gives church leaders and congregants media capabilities that are contemporary, relevant, effective, and, most importantly, affordable and sustainable.

With *Amplify Media* church leaders can:

+ Provide a reliable source of Christian content through a Wesleyan lens for teaching, training, and inspiration in a customizable library
+ Deliver their own preaching and worship content in a way the congregation knows and appreciates
+ Build the church's capacity to innovate with engaging content and accessible technology
+ Equip the congregation to better understand the Bible and its application
+ Deepen discipleship beyond the church walls

⋀ AMPLIFY™ MEDIA

Ask your group leader or pastor about Amplify Media and sign up today at www.AmplifyMedia.com.

Printed in the USA
CPSIA information can be obtained
at www.ICGtesting.com
LVHW030737271124
797494LV00005B/10